Above: *Bridge Street.*

About 20,000 people now live in Stratford. Over the centuries it has spread out from the medieval grid of stree at its centre to absorb its expanding population. In Shakespeare's day, however, this criss-cross of streets on west bank of the Avon comprised the whole of the town; according to contemporary surveys, about 2000 people live there in some 217 houses. There were plenty of trees and gardens and the surrounding fields and copses were never more than a minute or two's walk from any part of the tov Different livestock markets were held in different streets, though now they are all centralised in the Rother market still an important market for the local farmers.

Even without Shakespeare to boost its fame, Stratford would still be a major attraction for visitors. Its beautiful houses, gardens, church and river all make it one of the fir and most unspoilt market towns in England. The magnific parish church of the Holy Trinity, dating from the early thirteenth century, stands at the extreme south of the tov Its detached position is accounted for by the fact that it wa built on the site of a Saxon monastery, whereas the town itself grew up around the river crossing, certainly used by Romans and probably before that by the Celts.

Stratford actually takes its name from the ford of the street, or road, across the Avon. In the Middle Ages when Stratford developed as a trading centre, the ford was bridg over. The solid stone bridge which carries road traffic toda was built 500 years ago by a local man, Sir Hugh Clopton, and apart from a little widening and raising of the parapet, has changed little since the days of cart and packhorse.

Pleasure boats on the River Avon.

e: Clopton Bridge.

row boat on the River Avon.

Above: *The Dirty Duck Inn.*

Most of the existing timber-framed buildings in Stratford date from the seventeenth century. Three disastrous fires during Shakespeare's lifetime destroyed many of the older medieval structures – and the vulnerability of timber-framed buildings to fire makes it remarkable that so many have survived at all. Perhaps the finest example of rebuilding after these fires is Harvard House in the High Street. It is of special interest to Americans since it was the childhood home of the mother of John Harvard, one of the founders of the famous Harvard University in Massachusetts. It is now owned by the University.

From the late seventeenth century houses were increasingly built of or faced with brick and roofed with tile to reduce the hazard of fire. Stone has never been widely used as a building material in this part of the country because the nearest good source is in the Cotswold Hills, some distance away to the south.

The quality of Stratford's historic architecture is a clear sign of its prosperity in past times. Its wealth was derived from trade rather than manufacturing, mainly because its strategic position at the hub of a network of road and river communications made it a natural meeting place for merchants and dealers from outlying districts. The town received its first charter allowing it to hold a market in 119 and from that time its significance as a trading centre developed. First it was a local market for neighbouring farmers. Then it grew into a larger-scale market attended dealers from the manufacturing districts around Birmingh to the north and merchants from the rich agricultural countries to the south. It was well-known that the cheapes wheat and malt could always be got at Stratford.

Plenty of farmers still come to market in Stratford, whic is probably one reason why there are so many pubs in the town. Down at the Dirty Duck, however, you are more like to find actors and actresses from the Shakespeare Theatre across the road than sons of the soil from the farms.

After harvest every year the farm labourers and servant used to come into town for the hiring fair to find a new employer for the coming year. The fair, traditionally called the Stratford Mop, is still held every 12 October, but it is now more to do with having fun than finding a job.

Stalls at the Mop Fair.

Morris dan

...vard House.

The house where Shakespeare was born is in Henley Street. It is an early sixteenth-century timber-framed building standing on a low base wall of local stone. In Tudor times it was actually two separate houses. John Shakespeare, William's father, ran his successful glove-making and agricultural merchant's business in one, while in the other (the one with the porch at the front) he lived with his wife and family. Here it is believed that Shakespeare was born on 23 April 1564, a day celebrated in Stratford every year with folk dancing, receptions, speeches, toasts, processions and wreath-laying on Shakespeare's tomb. It has to be said, however, that there is no hard evidence either that the family were living in the house as early as this, or that Shakespeare was actually born on 23 April. What is certain is that he was baptised at the parish church of Holy Trinity on 26 April 1564. William was the first son born to the Shakespeares,

Above: *William Shakespeare by Soest.*

The Guildhall and Almshou

...ugh they already had two daughters, ...n and Margaret.

...he old house in Henley Street ...ained in the family after ...kespeare's death until the nineteenth ...tury. In 1847 it was bought by public ...scription and in 1891 turned over to ... Shakespeare Birthplace Trust to be ...served in perpetuity as Shakespeare's ...thplace. Naturally it underwent ...stantial alterations over the ...turies, but steps were taken in 1858 ...restore it as far as possible to ...nething approaching its original ...pearance. No one can be quite sure, ...wever, exactly what the house was ... when the Shakespeare family first ...d there.

...Very little is known of Shakespeare's ...ldhood or education. As one of the ...mbers of the town council, his father ...s entitled to free education for his ...ns at the grammar school and almost ...tainly this is where young William ...akespeare received his schooling. The ... grammar school room can still be ...n on the first floor of a block of ...cient timber-framed buildings next ...or to the church on the corner of ...urch Street and Chapel Lane. They ...re erected in the fifteenth century by ... Guild of the Holy Cross, a religious ...d social institution founded in 1269 ...ich virtually ran the town until ...placed by the town council during the ...formation. The much older Guild ...apel adjoining was also totally rebuilt ... the same time.

...A tradition of the local school, which ...ll uses the old school room, is that ...akespeare sat by a window at the ...rthern end and used the desk (or one ...e it) which is now preserved in the ...rthplace. Generations of pupils have ...t their names or initials carved into ...rious pieces of furniture, but ...akespeare's has not yet been found ...nong them.

Above: *Shakespeare's Birthplace in Henley Street.*

Above: *The room where Shakespeare was born.*

The Birthplace garden.

Above: *Anne Hathaway's Cottage, Shottery, in winter.*

In 1582 Shakespeare married Anne Hathaway, possibly under some duress since he was only 18 years old and she was already several months pregnant when the ceremony is said to have taken place. Eight years Shakespeare's senior Anne was the daughter of a prosperous farmer in the nearby village of Shottery.

The Hathaway farmhouse, formerly called Hewland Farm, is still standing and is known the world over from countless reproductions in books and calendars as Anne Hathaway's Cottage. The name is in fact somewhat misleading since the house is actually a substantial structure, dating from the fifteenth century. The Hathaways and their descendants continued to live there until 1892 when it was acquired by the Shakespeare Birthplace Trust. Some of the family's furniture is still in position after many hundreds of years, including the bed in which Anne's parents slept, and the settle by the fire on which Shakespeare is said to have wooed his bride. The picturesque, thickly-thatched house, set amidst orchards and well-kept cottage gardens, is a classic image of rural England.

William and Anne were probably married some time towards the end of 1582, although nobody knows the actual date or, indeed, the location of the ceremony. The village of Temple Grafton a few miles west of Shottery is generally thought to have been the most likely venue, although the old church at Luddington (long since replaced by a more recent structure) also has its supporters. Their first child, Susanna, was born in May 1583. The twins Hamnet and Judith appeared in February 1585.

The next we hear of Shakespeare is that he had moved to London and become an actor and a playwright. According to tradition, it was a result of an incident at Charlecote Park, near Stratford, that Shakespeare left family and friends in Stratford and went up to the capital to start a new life in the bohemian world of the theatre.

Inside Anne Hathaway's Cottage.

ve: *Anne Hathaway's Cottage in summer.*

River Avon at Charlecote.

A cottage at Shottery.

9

Above: *Deer in Charlecote Park.*

Apparently he was caught poaching in the deer park and was brought before the owner, Sir Thomas Lucy. Lucy also happened to be the local magistrate, a duly punished the offender. In reveng Shakespeare is said to have written a scurrilous verse about the magistrate which he pinned up on the gatehouse door at Charlecote. Such was Lucy's fury at his impudence that Shakespea had to leave the district altogether an thus ended up in London. However much this story may tax one's credulity, it is more or less certain tha Lucy was the model for the caricature Justice Shallow in the plays *The Merry Wives of Windsor* and *Henry IV, Part II.*

After a decade in London, separated from his family, back in Stratford, Shakespeare returned in 1597 and bought New Place, the largest house the town. Although only 33, Shakespeare had become a wealthy m on the proceeds of his acting and his writing. No doubt he was already looking for somewhere to invest his money, but the death of his 11-year-c son, Hamnet, the previous year may have been the immediate cause of his temporary return to his home town. continued performing and writing in London for some years to come.

Sited on the corner of Chapel Stree and Chapel Lane, opposite the Guild Chapel, the boundaries of the New Pl property are still as they were in Shakespeare's day, though the house itself is no longer standing. It is recor that it was 'a pretty house of brick an timber' built a century before by the same Sir Hugh Clopton who gave

The Knott Garden at New Place

ve: The dining room at Hall's Croft.

Stratford its bridge. It would no doubt have been standing today had it not been for the Rev. Francis Gastrell, an eighteenth century clergyman infamous to all Shakespeare lovers. Annoyed by the number of people asking permission to see the mulberry tree which Shakespeare planted in the New Place garden, he chopped it down and sold the wood to an enterprising local carver to be made into souvenirs. In 1759 following a dispute with the town authorities Gastrell went even further and pulled down the house itself. For this act of vandalism he was drummed out of the town 'amidst the rage and curses of its inhabitants'. All that can be seen of New Place now are some foundations, cellar walls and a well – and, of course, the gardens.

There are two gardens on the New Place site, the Knott Garden and the Great Garden. The Knott Garden, so called because of the complex pattern formed by the low hedges, is designed and planted as a replica of an Elizabethan garden. The dwarf hedges are made up of herbs mentioned in Shakespeare's plays. The Great Garden is a lovely open space in the centre of the town, ringed with tall old trees and neat borders, and protected by a high wall. As in the garden at the Birthplace, many of the plants which give life and colour to Shakespeare's plays are planted here, where perhaps the poet himself gardened from time to time.

dispensary at Hall's Croft.

Overleaf: *Hall's Croft from the garden.*

Above: *Holy Trinity Church.*

Left: *The bust of Shakespeare inside Holy Trinity Church.*

Hall's Croft is in the part of Stratford called the Old Town, between New Place and Holy Trinity Church. This fine Tudor house is named after Dr John Hall, a physician from Bedfordshire who settled in Stratford and married Shakespeare's eldest daughter Susanna in June 1607.

In 1608 the Halls had a daughter, Elizabeth, who married as her first husband Thomas Nash, the son of one of Shakespeare's Stratford friends. The Nashes lived in Nash's House, next door to New Place and now a fascinating Stratford and Shakespeare museum. High up on the side we can still be seen an inverted 'V' mark where the New Place gable abutted onto it. Nash's House is another timber-frame building with wattle and plaster infill, though the frontage quite modern.

Shakespeare's other daughter, Judith, married Thomas Quiney, of another family well known to Shakespeare. They lived in the white house (now the information centre) on the corner of Bridge Street and High Street, looking out on the spot where old John Shakespeare used to set out his glove stall on market days. Shakespeare's father died in September 1601, happily having lived long enough to see his son make good and restore the family's fortunes which had sunk to a low ebb after his glove business fell off in the 1570s.

Shortly after Judith's marriage in March 1616 Shakespeare fell seriously ill. A convivial man, the story goes that he had 'merry meeting' at New Place with fellow writers Ben Jonson and Michael Drayton as a result of which he contracted a deadly fever. It carried him off on 23 April 1616, his fifty-sixth birthday if the traditional date of his birth is correct.

On 25 April he was buried in Holy Trinity Church. The fact that he had invested some of his considerable wealth in buying half the tithes attached to the church meant that he and his family were entitled to burial plots within the chancel, hence the grave slabs of Anne, his wife (died 1623), Thomas Nash, Dr Hall and Susanna, his daughter, lined up before the altar.

On the north wall of the chancel there is a bust of Shakespeare, pen in hand, framed between two columns. Along with the engraving of Shakespeare in the First Folio his plays (published 1623) this statue has a claim to be one of the only two surviving portraits of Shakespeare known to have been executed within the lifetime of people who knew him intimately. As such they have pretensions to be reasonable likenesses. The monument was installed in the church in 1623.

e: Holy Trinity graveyard.

GOOD FREND FOR IESVS SAKE. FORBEARE,
TO DIGG THE DVST ENCLOASED HEARE:
BLESE BE Y MAN Y SPARES HES STONES,
AND CVRST BE HE Y MOVES MY BONES.

kespeare's grave inside Holy Trinity Church.

There is a much larger, seated statue
Shakespeare in the Bancroft Gardens
which was presented by its designer,
Lord Robert Sutherland Gower, in 18
But perhaps the greatest monument
the man is the Royal Shakespeare
Theatre on the banks of the Avon. A
theatre was first erected on this site
1879, but it burnt down in 1926. The
present building was opened in 1932.
Here Shakespeare's plays, some of
which he probably conceived and wrd
just a step or two away at New Place
continue to be performed and enjoye
by thousands.

Opinions differ as to whether the
building suits its surroundings, but
there is no doubt that from the point
view of putting on plays the interior
superbly designed. Next door is the
Swan Theatre, built along the lines o
typical Elizabethan playhouse and
intended for the presentation of play
contemporaries of Shakespeare. It w
opened in 1986.

Above: *The Royal Shakespeare Theatre.*

A performance of The Taming of the Sh

e: *The Swan Theatre.*

Avon and the Shakespeare Theatre.

The statue of Hamlet on the Gower Memorial.

17

Shakespeare may have been brought up as a town-dweller, but his parents and ancestors on both sides were country people. Before moving to Stratford around 1550 Shakespeare's father lived in Snitterfield, a village a few miles north-east of Stratford where *his* father, Richard Shakespeare, was a tenant farmer. Shakespeare's mother, Mary Arden, came from another village nearby. She was the youngest daughter of Robert Arden of Wilmcote, a small landowner and head of a minor branch of Warwickshire gentry prominent in the county at that time.

The Ardens' beautiful old manor house, with its barns, duckpond and late fifteenth century dovecote, still stands at Wilmcote, now preserved for posterity by the Shakespeare Birthplace Trust. Until as recently as 1930 it was a working farm and now it houses a large collection of old farm implements.

Robert Arden was Richard Shakespeare's landlord at Snitterfield, and this is presumably how John Shakespeare got to know Mary. They married in 1557. No record exists of the ceremony, but it probably took place at Aston Cantlow church, also the parish church of Wilmcote.

The countryside around Stratford where Shakespeare's ancestors farmed is without question among the loveliest in England. It is a rich historic landscape of rolling hills, mature woods and fertile farmland, dotted with picturesque manor houses and beautiful old villages of characteristic black-and-white architecture. Shakespeare must have travelled over this area many times and come to know it intimately. It is now so closely identified with his life and work that it has been dubbed 'Shakespeare Country'. It feels like the heart of England – and it is no surprise to find that geographically it very nearly is.

To the north is Warwick, another old medieval town about the same size as Stratford, but altogether different in character because of its historic role as a military and administrative centre. It is dominated by its massive medieval castle, built on a buttress of rock on the banks of the Avon. For centuries the home of the Earls of Warwick, it was until recently the oldest inhabited medieval fortress in the country. Madame Tussaud's of London now runs it as a museum and a branch of the famous waxworks.

Above: *Mary Arden's House, Wilmcote.*

Inside Mary Arden's House.

ve: *The town of Warwick overshadowed by the Castle.*

Above: *Warwick Castle.*

n Cantlow.

The finest timber-framed building in Warwick is Lord Leycester's Hospital. Once in the joint possession of two medieval guilds, the building was converted into housing for wounded ex-soldiers by Robert Dudley, Earl of Leicester, in 1571. Four hundred years on, it still provides accommodation for ex-servicemen 'hurt in the wars'.

In complete contrast to ancient Warwick, Royal Leamington Spa is a gracious Regency town of wide streets and elegant stuccoed houses. Until the late eighteenth century it was an obscure village, but then the discovery of medicinal springs there led to its rapid growth as a fashionable spa town. It has now merged with Warwick into one built-up area.

In the south of the Shakespeare country, Chipping Campden is an old town that blends so perfectly with its surroundings that it seems to have grown quite naturally out of the ground rather than to have been built. Chipping Campden is much smaller than Stratford or Warwick, but it has an illustrious history economically.

In the Middle Ages it was the centre of the lucrative wool trade. Many rich merchants lived here, including William Grevel, described on his memorial brass in the church as 'the flower of the wool merchants of all England'. Grevel died in 1401, but his house still adorns Chipping Campden's matchless High Street.

The market hall in the High Street was built in 1627 by Sir Baptist Hicks to house the poultry, butter and cheese market. It is now owned by the National Trust, which looks after so many historic properties in this area.

The Shakespeare country is bordered on the south by the northern edge of the Cotswold hills. In the east is Edge Hill, over 700 feet (200 metres) high, where one of the bloodiest battles of the Civil War was fought in 1642. To the west is Broadway Hill, rising over 1000 feet (300 metres) above the village of Broadway. On top of the hill stands Broadway Tower, built by the Earl of Coventry at the end of the eighteenth century – for no other reason than to gratify a whim of his wife's. On a clear day you can see 13 different counties from the top of the tower.

Above: *Lord Leycester's Hospital, Warwick.*

The tomb of Robert Dudley in St Mary's Church, Warwick.

Chipping Campden, Gloucestershire.

ve: Broadway Tower on Broadway Hill.

w towards Broadway from Broadway Hill.

Above: *The moat at Baddesley Clinton.*

Ragley Hall in Warwicks.

ry village in this special part of England has some
hitectural gem to boast of, whether it be a church or just a
ple country cottage. Welford-on-Avon, for example, has
e lovely half-timbered houses, not to mention its oak
gate – through which churchgoers have been passing for
last four centuries – and its striped maypole, said to be
highest in the country.

ike any rural area, there are numerous country houses
ng behind parks and woods, but what is remarkable about
Shakespeare country is the sheer variety of periods and
es represented in what is after all a comparatively small
. On the one hand, for example, there is Baddesley
nton, a romantic, moated, semi-fortified manor house
ng from the fifteenth century. On the other is Ragley
l, the classical eighteenth-century home of the Marquess
Hertford.

ear Ragley is Coughton Court, the ancestral home of the
rockmorton family, staunch Catholics and inveterate
ters during Shakespeare's lifetime. The building was
un about 1500, and the gatehouse completed about a
ade later. It was here that the wives and families of the
npowder Plotters anxiously waited to hear the fate of the
spirators in London.

wo houses are notable for their gardens. Packwood House
a mid-seventeenth century yew garden planted to
resent the Sermon on the Mount. A team of seven spends
nty days each year clipping the master, four evangelists,
lve apostles and the multitude on the lawn. The Tudor
se itself is worth seeing as well, particularly its splendid
at Hall open to a steeply-pitched roof with a minstrel's
ery at one end.

he garden at Hidcote is not only beautiful but botanically
nificant. Begun by Lawrence Johnstone, an American, in
7, it is actually a series of small gardens each devoted to a
ticular kind of flower. Rare plants and shrubs have been
ught to the garden from all over the world and some
eties grown there have been given the name 'Hidcote'.
ere is a veneration here for plants and flowers of which
kespeare, with his deep knowledge of the natural world,
uld certainly have approved.

Above: *Coughton Court, Warwickshire.*

ages at Welford-on-Avon, Warwickshire.

Topiary at Packwood House in Warwickshire.

23

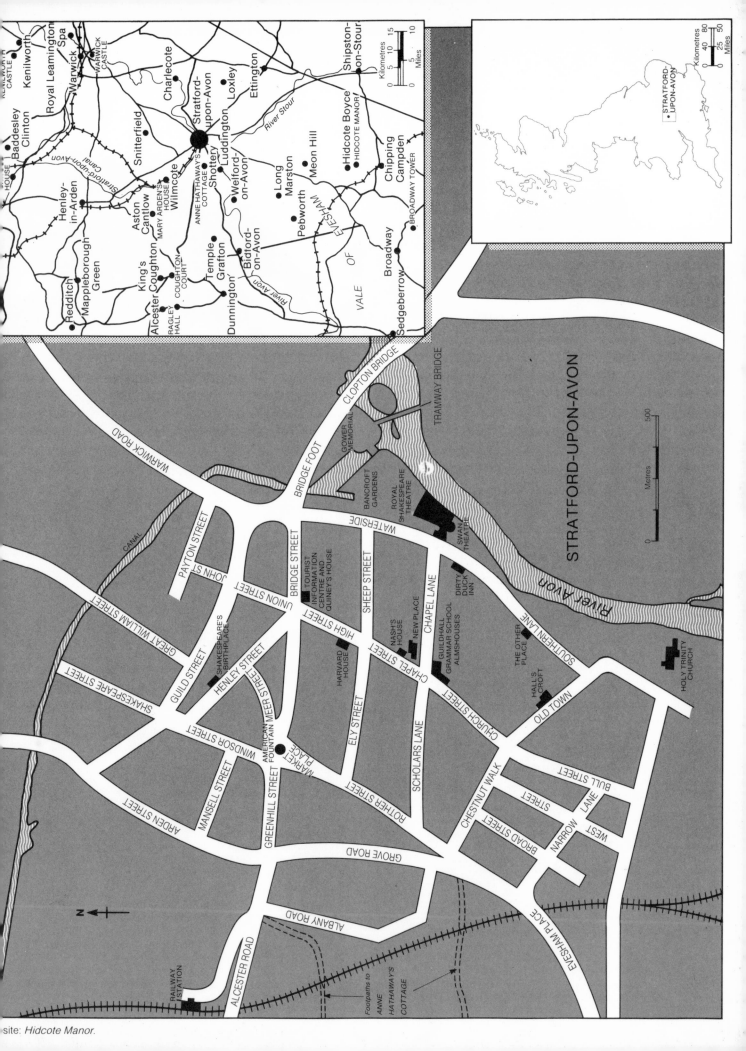

KENILWORTH CASTLE
Kenilworth
Royal Leamington Spa
Warwick
WARWICK CASTLE
Charlecote
Snitterfield
Stratford-upon-Avon
Loxley
Ettington
Shipston-on-Stour
River Stour

Baddesley Clinton
HOUSE
Stratford-upon-Avon Canal
Henley-in-Arden
Aston Cantlow
MARY ARDEN'S HOUSE
Wilmcote
ANNE HATHAWAY'S COTTAGE
Shottery
Luddington
Welford-on-Avon
Long Marston
Meon Hill
Hidcote Boyce
HIDCOTE MANOR!
Chipping Campden
BROADWAY TOWER

Redditch
Mappleborough Green
King's Coughton
Alcester
COUGHTON COURT
Temple Grafton
Dunnington
RAGLEY HALL
Bidford-on-Avon
Pebworth
River Avon
VALE OF EVESHAM
Broadway
Sedgeberrow

Kilometres 0 5 10 15
Miles 0 5 10

STRATFORD-UPON-AVON

Kilometres 0 40 80
Miles 0 25 50

STRATFORD-UPON-AVON

N

STRATFORD-UPON-AVON

Metres 0 500

CLOPTON BRIDGE
TRAMWAY BRIDGE
GOWER MEMORIAL
BANCROFT GARDENS
ROYAL SHAKESPEARE THEATRE
SWAN THEATRE
River Avon

WARWICK ROAD
BRIDGE FOOT
WATERSIDE
CANAL
PAYTON STREET
JOHN ST
BRIDGE STREET
UNION STREET
SHEEP STREET
DIRTY DUCK INN
SOUTHERN LANE

GREAT WILLIAM STREET
SHAKESPEARE'S BIRTHPLACE
HENLEY STREET
HIGH STREET
TOURIST INFORMATION CENTRE AND QUINEY'S HOUSE
NASH'S HOUSE
NEW PLACE
CHAPEL LANE
GUILDHALL GRAMMAR SCHOOL ALMSHOUSES
THE OTHER PLACE

SHAKESPEARE STREET
GUILD STREET
HARVARD HOUSE
CHAPEL STREET
CHURCH STREET
HALL'S CROFT
OLD TOWN
HOLY TRINITY CHURCH

MANSELL STREET
WINDSOR STREET
MEER STREET
AMERICAN FOUNTAIN
MARKET PLACE
ELY STREET
SCHOLARS LANE
CHESTNUT WALK
BROAD STREET
NARROW LANE
WEST STREET
BULL STREET

ARDEN STREET
GREENHILL STREET
ROTHER STREET
GROVE ROAD

ALBANY ROAD
ALCESTER ROAD
RAILWAY STATION
EVESHAM PLACE

Footpaths to ANNE HATHAWAY'S COTTAGE

site: Hidcote Manor.

STRATFORD-UPON-AVON

Set in the heart of England, Stratford-upon-Avon is
renowned the world over as the birthplace of William
Shakespeare. In this full-colour souvenir guide,
illustrated with over 50 superb photographs, William
Caldecott tells the story of Shakespeare in Stratford and
describes the town and the lovely 'Shakespeare country'
all around. A detailed map shows the location of major
sights and attractions.

STRATFORD

ISBN 1-85368-029-X

9 781853 680298

£2.

Trainer's Guide

caring for
preschool children *third edition*

Diane Trister Dodge • **Derry G. Koralek** • **Laurie Taub** • **Debra Al-Salam**